PTSD In Children Growing Up And Its Influences On Adult Life

by Orla Kelly

ISBN-13: 978-1514158258

ISBN-10: 1514158256

Contents

Overview

Today many children in our world are given little chance and opportunity to simply be a child. Instead they have learned through experience or through learning that the world can be a dangerous place where their security and safety are under threat. They feel alone, unsupported, neglected, unloved, and unsure of what to say or do, unable to articulate constructively how they feel or what the repercussions may be if they do! Children are growing up today absolutely traumatized by overwhelming events which have exceeded their capacity to cope and are at high risk of developing PTSD.

Historically PTSD was associated with returning war veterans and never a childhood condition. However children are very much at risk from a number of sources and if left untreated and inadequately managed, the likelihood of these children growing to adulthood as traumatized dysfunctional adults is enormous. Unfortunately, we may not be able to change human nature, but once we understand the unnecessary price paid by millions of innocent children, we may be better able to treat their wounds.

"Each day of our lives we make deposits in the memory banks of our children." Charles R. Swindoll

History and Risk Factors Associated with PTSD in Children

"I swore never to be silent whenever and wherever human beings endure suffering and humiliation. We must always take sides. Neutrality helps the oppressor, never the victim. Silence encourages the tormentor, never the tormented." Elie Wiesel

In looking at the history and risk factors associated with PTSD, it is important to first look at what determines whether a child has PTSD or not. There are a number of criteria which must be fulfilled for a diagnosis of PTSD and these are outlined in the Diagnostic and Statistical Manual of Mental Disorders (DSM) which is a manual containing the standard classification of mental disorders used by mental health professionals in the United States.

In this manual, it says that individuals can only develop PTSD if they have been exposed to a traumatic event where traumatic events "involve actual or threatened death or serious injury, or a threat to the physical integrity of oneself or others." This is found under the A1 criterion of the manual.

In addition, the individual's response must involve an intense emotional reaction such as fear, helplessness, or horror and is the A2 criterion. However, clinicians are now realizing that this is not always the case, as depending on the type of trauma and events around the trauma, this may not always occur.

The next criterion, the B criterion, addresses how PTSD can persist for extensive time periods and manifest itself as a re-experiencing and re-construction of events in the form of nightmares and flashbacks where terror is relived over and over.

The next criterion "C" addresses avoidance or the numbing response of an individual, involving strategies of a behavioral, cognitive, or emotional form, where the individual attempts to cope with what he or she has been traumatized by. They do this by trying to protect themselves from exposure to anything that would be considered a "trauma-related stimuli. Where avoidance is impossible or unlikely for the individual, they will try to numb themselves to minimize the intensity of their psychological reaction.

Criterion "D" addresses the "fight or flight" response, where an individual remains in a state of high alert, where they repeatedly scan their environment for stressors and risks. They anticipate danger and are always on the look- out and are afraid to let their guard down. Even things, places and events that would not normally be stressful, now take on a more sinister meaning. All this stress and tension can cause insomnia, mood swings and an inability to concentrate, as they may be unable to focus on just one thing. They can be very reactionary and easily startled. Again this is all part of the "fight or flight" response.

The "E" criterion involves the duration that PTSD symptoms must persist for. This was determined to be for at least one month.

Finally, the "F" criterion addresses the wider impact of PTSD, and how it impacts on the quality of life from all angles.

To date the majority of studies on PTSD have focused on military veterans, survivors of sexual assault, and survivors of natural disasters. Unfortunately there have been far less studies on exposure to violence, abuse and other traumas. While it is impossible to predict which child will get PTSD in response to trauma, studies have shown that there are a number of criteria which increase the likelihood of getting PTSD.

One of these is <u>resilience factors</u>, which are effectively protective factors of an environmental, cognitive and neurophysiological variety which help a child adapt and cope with trauma. There are also <u>genetic, biological, physiological, psychological and environmental variables</u>; which may increase vulnerability or predisposition to PTSD.

To summarize some of these studies, it has been found, that where certain <u>genetic factor vulnerabilities</u> exist, and in the presence of certain environmental factors, that there is a greater incidence of psychopathology. For example, persons with the long version of the gene coding of Monoamine Oxidase A (MOA), were found to be less susceptible to violence and be less aggressive than their peers with the short form of the gene.

Also where a person suffering from anxiety disorder had monozygotic twins, there was a greater likelihood that these twins would also go on to have anxiety disorders, indicating a genetic link to some PTSD related disorders.

<u>Biological factors</u> include elevated levels of cortisol which is associated with stress enhancing and thus increasing the predisposition to PTSD, while other individuals who have higher levels of chemicals called Dehydroepiandrosterone (DHEAS) which has the opposite effect to cortisol were less susceptible to PTSD.

<u>Physiological factors</u> which are associated with PTSD, include studies on the anterior cingulate and dorsolateral prefrontal areas of the brain. The former is associated with emotional processing and active memory function and the latter with the cognitive regulation and modulation to stress.

Other examples include an overactive hypothalamic pituary adrenal axis, which manifests itself cognitively and behaviorally in some of the characteristics evident in PTSD, such as stress, moods, emotions, and living out of a reactionary state or a state of emotional numbness. Studies also indicate a connection between a smaller than average hippocampus and PTSD but this is still inconclusive at present.

Examples of psychological factors include the level of a child's resilience. Where resilience is high, they are able to perform with a high level of executive function and cognitively process effectively what has happened. In addition, children with a positive temperament and disposition are better able to deal with challenges and cope better with stressful situations. The opposite is also true where resilience is low.

Environmental factors play a critical role in PTSD incidence for children. Children growing up in high risk environments have a greater chance of getting PTSD than those in low environmental risk areas. This was found to be regardless of the level of the individual's resilience factors. The level of parental and social support were critical components of the risk assessment. Other key environmental factors were, whether the trauma was once off or repeated, chronic vs acute and whether the child was exposed to other traumas.

Regarding the above, some of the criteria for PTSD will not be relevant for some children while others will be very relevant. This is because there are so many different means by which a child can get PTSD.

When looking further at specific risk factors for PTSD, they can be divided into three subgroups.

These include pre-traumatic, traumatic, and post-traumatic factors. Examples of pre-traumatic risk factors include poverty, family psychiatric history, other childhood traumas and behavior, family support structure etc. and these factors set the scene for PTSD to occur. The next traumatic factors involve the actual trauma. Finally the post-traumatic environment plays a significant role in later development of PTSD, where children's needs "post trauma" are not met either in the home or outside the home.

How a child will cope with trauma will depend on the following factors:

- Type of trauma

- Severity of the trauma

- Previous exposure to trauma and incidence of trauma event or events

- Family history of psychological or other problems

- Reaction of parents to the trauma and family support

- Proximity of the child to the trauma

- Duration of trauma event or events

- Age of the child

- Levels of and extent of resilience factors present in the child

- Level of existing coping skills for dealing with conflict and trauma.

- How the child deals with anxiety and situations that bring about distress

- How they deal with uncertainty and unpredictability

- How they regulate and express their emotions

Type of Trauma

The type of trauma experienced or witnessed by a child, plays a large part in determining whether the child will go on to develop PTSD or not.

Some examples of trauma events include where the child perceives there is a direct threat to their life or personal safety, or to the life or safety of a loved one.

It also includes where there is intentional severe harm in the form of rape, physical assault or torture and these events tend to give rise to greater incidences of PTSD. Also where a child is caught totally off guard and unaware of what was going to happen, and if they felt totally overwhelmed, unable to escape and helpless, these events are more traumatic for the child. All these considerations play a significant role in the potential for PTSD to occur.

It isn't just a direct experience of something horrific that gives rise to PTSD. Witnessing something traumatic happen to someone the child feels close to, or even finding out that something traumatic happened to a loved one can give rise to PTSD.

Some examples of this would be:

1. Sexual, emotional and physical abuse or severe neglect,

2. Severe bullying, violent crimes or violence in the community or school setting,

3. A car accident or other event where a person close to the child gets injured or killed,

4. Undergoing major surgery, hospitalization, disfigurement or other serious condition of a life changing nature,e.g cancer or asthma,

5. Witnessing the lives of parents or others close to the child, spiral out of control due to alcohol, drugs, mental health problems etc.,

6. Witnessing a parent or sibling being abused or assaulted,

7. Hearing about a friend or family member's suicide,

8. Getting caught up in natural disasters such as hurricanes, earthquakes, tsunamis, storms, fires, floods etc. and witnessing devastation and destruction,

9. Having a parent killed or injured in war,

10. Living in a home where a parent has PTSD.

Even though trauma can be brought directly into a child's home via all forms of media, this will have a far lesser impact on children than if they are actually witnessing or experiencing the event.

The more severe the trauma, the greater potential for PTSD to occur. Whether the child was injured or witnessed another person who is emotionally close to them getting injured or killed in traumatic or violent unexpected circumstances or even hearing about a major traumatic event happening to a loved one, can result in the child becoming traumatized, feeling intense fear and helplessness and being unable to understand or process what has happened.

The more a child is exposed to trauma or repeated traumatic events, the greater the likelihood for PTSD to develop. This is because, over time, the child will view him or herself differently, see others differently, respond to the world differently and live in fear because of what they have experienced and how it translates in their understanding of events.

Family history plays a major role in how a child will respond to a traumatic event. For example, if a parent is suffering from PTSD, depression, acute anxiety, substance or alcohol abuse or other illnesses, it will impact their duty of care to their child. Where a parent or caregiver is unable to fulfil their role as parent and guardian, children grow up with destructive beliefs and feel the world is a dangerous place where they cannot rely on their parents to protect them.

How the parents react to the trauma witnessed or experienced by the child and the level of family support that exists is a significant factor for PTSD. Where parents can support, reassure, nurture and talk things through with a child and listen and respond to them in an empathetic and positively reinforcing manner, the child has a greater chance of being able to work things through in their mind. They will also be able to process their feelings and emotions in a healthy constructive way.

Family support from other family members outside of parents can also assist the child in coming to terms with what has happened. Sometimes parents may react emotionally and be so overcome with grief and emotion that they may not be able to deal with their own feelings and those of the child, and so other family members can step in to help out. Some examples can include grandparents, aunts, uncles, older cousins etc.

Another factor is how physically close the child was to the trauma as it was unfolding. Children who were up close to the trauma were found to be most negatively impacted by the trauma, rather than children who had some distance between them and the trauma. The child is so close to the event with little else to distract them from the horror they are witnessing.

The duration of the trauma event and frequency of any repeat events serve to reinforce the trauma experience for the child, and each time it is relived, the potential for PTSD increases. A child may not get PTSD the first time they experience trauma, but repeat traumas serve to increase in the child, a sense that they are in danger again. The more a child believes they are in danger, the more traumatized they will be. No matter how traumatic one-time traumas are, prolonged and repeated traumatic experiences result in the most serious mental health problems including PTSD.

The age of the child also plays a role in PTSD, as it is believed that children of different ages respond differently to PTSD. This is discussed in more detail in this book.

How resilient a child is before being subjected to trauma, goes a long way in determining whether they will be likely to get PTSD. Resilience really comes down to the coping skills a child has developed to help them through trauma and conflict. This is personal and really is down to a child's life experiences, thoughts, beliefs and support systems in place.

Some examples would be how well a child can deal with unpredictability and uncertainty in their life, how they deal with stress, anxiety and any problems as they occur, and how they express themselves and their emotions.

If a child is sensitive to their environment and tends to suffer from anxiety when faced with new situations or situations they feel are outside their control, they will be more vulnerable to PTSD. So also if they believe they are at risk when faced with uncertainty and unpredictability, they will tend to worry more and feel things are outside their control, and they are powerless. All this build- up of negative emotion will cause distress, even in situations which would not be particularly stressful.

After any negative experiences, how a child processes their emotions, will determine if their response is healthy or unhealthy to any event that causes distress. If their tolerance to emotional distress is low, they have a greater potential for PTSD.

In looking at PTSD in children, the following scenarios are reviewed:

1. Children experiencing direct personal trauma giving rise to PTSD

2. Children experiencing trauma by witnessing a significant trauma incident or event

3. Children becoming traumatized by having someone close to them

with a serious life threatening condition, being harmed or killed

4. Children experiencing trauma by inheriting their parents PTSD trauma or experiencing direct trauma inflicted due to some of the side effects of their parent suffering from PTSD

5. Children growing up in a dysfunctional household where there was significant neglect (lack of care and lack of provision of basic human rights), abuse (sexual, physical, mental, verbal) giving rise to PTSD. This could be from substance or alcohol abuse, mental health problems, significant lack of parenting skills etc. in the household.

These scenarios are discussed throughout this book.

PTSD Symptoms For Different Age Groups Of Children

"All the world is full of suffering. It is also full of overcoming." Helen Keller

A child can experience PTSD at any age, and its onset can be immediate or gradually over time. If it does occur, the symptoms generally appear within 3 months and last longer than one month. Unfortunately due to many factors, it can last for a very long time or go away and then come back again when triggered by something the child finds traumatic. The criteria used to diagnose PTSD is given in the first Chapter.

The following is a list of some of the most common PTSD symptoms that children experience:

1. Ongoing nightmares

2. Insomnia

3. Fear

4. Being irritable or aggressive and prone to anger outbursts

5. Hyper vigilance

6. Social withdrawal and isolation

7. Separation anxiety

8. Diminished performance in school and other activities and loss of interest thereof

9. Emotionally numb

10. Difficulty concentrating and focusing

11. Guilt

12. Anxiety

13. Reporting physical illnesses

Children tend to exhibit symptoms of PTSD a little differently to adults.

For younger children

1. Younger children may not exhibit many outward signs of PTSD other than maybe being more fearful, anxious and fretful about being separated from someone they trust.

2. They may begin to fear people whom they would have been previously been very comfortable around.

3. They may try to avoid doing things they once enjoyed or normally participated in. This includes going to the playground, going to school, visiting family or friends, going to the grocery store etc. Instead they may prefer to stay at home and they may be very particular with whom they want around them.

4. They may engage in a form of play where they re-create traumatic events, but this would not be constructive play that allows them to process what has happened, and help them move on from the trauma, but instead keeps them locked in the situation where events are repeated over and over, serving to remind them and reinforce what happened.

5. They may begin to act as if younger than their years, by regressing,

and may start using "baby voices" and language, not wanting to do things they could do such as feeding themselves, dressing, toileting etc.

6. They may experience nightmares and disturbed sleep.

7. They may become easily anxious and fretful even over things that never caused concern in the past.

For older kids of school going age

They will interpret what happened differently to adults and may put the order of traumatic events together in the wrong sequence. They may also put the wrong type of information together and give relevance to something which may have been irrelevant to the event that took place.

Typical Examples

*   If it was night time when the trauma occurred or a certain day, month etc. They may think this is an important factor in the trauma, whereas, it will most likely be irrelevant. They will then continue to look for signs that would indicate the trauma would re-occur and would be in a state of vigilance and high alert during these times.

*   They may also recreate events that were similar to those where the trauma occurred, but this does not bring comfort or closure to the child, but it is a reliving of the experience or event for the child, and does not help ease any anxiety experienced.

*   They may also develop sleep problems and nightmares and develop new phobias.

*   They may report aches and pains but there may be no physical reason for them.

- They may have difficulty concentrating at school and be easily distracted or startled.

For Teenagers

- Some teenagers begin to experience symptoms of PTSD comparable with those of adults but will differ in some respects.

- They may feel deeply about what happened and question themselves if they could have done more to prevent the situation, and blame themselves for what happened in the first place. They may experience a lot of guilt around this.

- They may experience flashbacks and get very upset and not want to talk about it, or if they do, they may talk about looking for revenge and not speak rationally.

- They may get nightmares and have trouble sleeping.

- They may begin to avoid situations that were once familiar and safe and regress emotionally and behaviorally and be more prone to temper outbursts.

- They may dabble in recreational drugs, alcohol or substance abuse and hang out with the wrong crowd where they may get into trouble with the law or within their communities, school etc.

- They will find it harder to regulate their emotional response and tend to be more impulsive and aggressive when suffering from PTSD.

- They may push boundaries, lash out, and be more rebellious, disrespectful and may go down a self-destructive path or engage in more destructive behavior of a general nature.

- They may have difficulty concentrating at school and be easily distracted or startled.

- They may become emotionally withdrawn and find it hard to maintain contact with others, or the reverse may happen and they may become very clingy.

- Depending on the trauma they may feel embarrassed or ashamed or very sad.

Children can also develop secondary PTSD. Although there is a significant overlap between primary and secondary PTSD, **there are some symptoms that are most prevalent in children whose parent has PTSD.**

- Believing they are to blame for a parent's PTSD symptoms;

- Believing their parent no longer cares about them or loves them anymore;

- Trying to re-connect and find common ground with their parent by mimicking their parent's attitude and actions;

- Trying to fill all the gaps in their lives by trying to do everything neglected by the parent to make life feel normal for themselves, even if it sometimes means they try to fill their parents place;

Other common symptoms are:

1. Extreme mood swings and acting up, often quite aggressively

2. Depression and anxiety;

3. Lack of interest in friends activities and past times

4. Isolation and withdrawal;

5. More engagement in fights and arguments in the home and harming

of siblings;

6. Self-destruction or destruction of property;

7. Falling behind in course work and grades at school;

8. Difficulty maintaining and developing friendships;

In terms of symptoms, it is found that interpersonal trauma, where trauma is inflicted on the child by another person had a significantly greater likelihood of PTSD occurrence and the symptoms of trauma were more severe than from natural disasters, accidents and the like. Some examples of this include sexual abuse, physical abuse and violence. These are discussed in more details in the following chapters.

Children Suffering Personal Trauma Or Witnessing Trauma Of A Loved One

"Our prime purpose in this life is to help others. And if you can't help them, at least don't hurt them." Dalai Lama

There are so many events and circumstances that can give rise to PTSD in a child. These include, abuse of all forms, undergoing a major illness, being involved in a car crash, getting caught up in a natural disaster, being severely bullied, living in a war torn region etc.

There are millions of displaced and traumatized children growing up around the world without members of their family who are either fighting in a war or who are missing or murdered, who are displaced, who are without their home, without education, often with inadequate food, shelter and basic humanitarian supplies which are in short supply, or which are being denied to them due to ongoing sanctions by government bodies. They are also dealing with totally inadequate services to help them cope with everything that they have experienced. These children are growing up living in fear, living in an environment that has stripped them of their childhood and of their rights to be a child.

Humanitarian services are overstretched and there is a significant amount of aid not reaching children who most need it, and what does reach them is often insufficient. Unless something is done now for these children, the likelihood is, that they will grow up to be traumatized angry adults, who will most likely suffer from PTSD. For as long as there will be wars and humanitarian sanctions, children will continue to suffer and ultimately we will all pay a heavy price for this injustice and travesty.

Natural disasters such as terrifying storms, hurricanes, floods, earthquakes and tremors can give rise to a great deal of stress for children as they may have to deal with being displaced from their home, having their home and belongings lost, being separated from their loved ones and not knowing if they came to harm or were killed until sometime later. They may see their communities destroyed, and maybe then experiencing violence in the chaos there after, are also things that can give rise to PTSD in children. They may become more fretful and anxious, afraid to sleep, afraid to part from a parents company, lash out at others or regress in many ways as they struggle to come to terms with what happened.

When a child develops a major or life threatening illness, advances in medical intervention and technology help more children survive with these illnesses, but there can be long lasting negative effects that can impact on the mental health of the child. Some examples include cancer, chronic asthma and other debilitating illnesses.

Every year, thousands of children and their families are affected by cancer. Not only is the child coping with the illness and how it affects their body, but they may be also dealing with pain, side effects from medication and medical interventions, and the stress all this puts on their body.

Children are living with the stress of a diagnosis and then living with the illness and treatment thereof. Living with a fear of the unknown and of what may happen to them and what the future may hold, can be very traumatic for a child.

Even if a child does not develop PTSD, they many still experience some symptoms of PTSD.

While there seems to be greater number of girls than boys who survive childhood cancer, going on to develop PTSD, other risk factors associated with PTSD such as poor family and social support, and other stressful events going on in the child's life also increase the child's risk from PTSD.

Asthma is another potentially life threatening illness and can result in death also. It is also one of the most common reasons why children are hospitalized each year. The unexpected nature of an asthma attack, and the frightening physical symptoms that are associated with an asthma attack, instil fear and helplessness and a fear of the unknown and can give rise to PTSD.

The severity of the illness seems to play a lesser role in PTSD development, rather than the role that psychological factors seem to play, in looking at the risk for developing PTSD.

Another factor that many children have to deal with, is bullying. Bullying can be defined as a repeated and intentional act of aggression, where one or more people plan to harm or upset another person physically, verbally, or psychologically. Although bullying in itself albeit stressful, and may even give rise to some symptoms of PTSD for the child, it generally isn't enough to give rise to PTSD. However extreme bullying where the child strongly believes his or her life is in danger, or that they will come to serious injury, can give rise to PTSD where the child reacts with fear, helplessness or horror.

Being involved in a car crash can also give rise to PTSD and the child may play back over and over the events in their mind or through play but not in a way that is constructive. They may even blame themselves for what happened and recall vividly the sound of the impact, injuries experienced etc. They may remain fearful of traveling again in a car and remain trapped in their negative emotions around what happened.

A number of children who may witness the effects of terrorist attacks are susceptible to PTSD but it is believed that they are more likely to experience symptoms of PTSD such as re-experiencing events or hyper arousal, rather than a full diagnosis of PTSD. This is believed to be because they may be sheltered by their families from witnessing the horrors or from watching the news and also younger children would have less of an understanding of what was happening.

Where children are subjected to abuse of a sexual (including rape), physical, verbal or psychological nature they have a greater chance of getting PTSD, particularly if the abuse is ongoing. The effects can be even more damaging when it is a caregiver or a person the child has trusted and looked up to.

Studies have shown that adults who have experienced abuse of a physical, sexual and emotional nature while a child, show greater tendencies to be abusive in close relationships and are more likely to be diagnosed with PTSD.

PTSD in children can also occur where there is an unexpected or violent death of a family member or someone close to them, or where there is serious injury, harm or serious illness and a near death experience of a loved one. Where children experience a greater than normal sadness and reaction to the above, they are said to suffer from childhood traumatic grief. Part of this involves symptoms comparable to PTSD such as avoidance, re-experiencing and hyper arousal.

They may have intrusive memories and nightmares about the death of their loved one, they may emotionally withdraw and refuse to talk about the person who died and how they died, or they may develop symptoms such as decreased concentration, reported aches and pains, become more fearful and anxious about their safety and wellbeing and of those close to them, become more irritable and prone to outbursts.

Children Inheriting Parental Trauma

"There are only two lasting bequests we can hope to give our children. One of these is roots, the other, wings." Johann Wolfgang von Goethe

Living with Parents with PTSD

When parents suffer from post-traumatic stress, whether it is long term or short term, it will affect the children too but the level by which they will be effected is down to a number of factors.

Children, especially in their younger years, learn by imitating their parents. Therefore, many of the negative and limiting behavior traits of parents with PTSD, are unintentionally instilled in their children, affecting their developmental, social and interpersonal skills. Children begin to display traits of their parents, believing what they are seeing and doing is normal acceptable behavior.

Of course no parent intentionally sets out to hurt or damage their child at any level in any way, but unfortunately their PTSD problems can get in the way of providing their children with the emotional and developmental support they need, and their need to grow up in a stable and nurturing home. Sadly this is denied to many children regardless of whether their parents have PTSD or not.

Unfortunately as children grow up in such an environment, they may consider the abnormal behavior of their parent as standard and learn to follow them, never knowing that what they are learning and imitating may be far from normal. It is often not until these children have grown up that they begin to feel something amiss, but it can be hard for them to pinpoint exactly what is different.

A child may feel responsible for what happened to their parent and feel they are to blame and are the cause of their parents' unhappiness and turmoil.

Parents who show traits of violence or depression as a result of post-traumatic stress, are more likely to pass on similar stress to their children, and as children learn from their parents, there is a greater likelihood they will continue this legacy of violence in their own lives. Where there are a number of children in the same family, one or more children may act out or behave aggressively towards their siblings as a way of mimicking their parent and trying to get attention.

Some parents suffering from PTSD are unable to go back to work or maintain gainful employment, thus creating a sense of instability and financial imbalance in their families lives. Living with financial instability as a normal part of their lives will also add to the stress of the child.

As a child, it is hard to understand and cope with a parent with PTSD. The air of secrecy and avoidance may be there, and children no matter how young they may be, can sense when a parent is unhappy or in a bad mood. Unable to understand the specific problem themselves, or do anything about their parent's misery, they often feel helpless and unwanted. They learn to hate the situation, then they may end up hating their parent, and finally they begins to hate themselves for hating their parent!

They may feel neglected, surplus to requirements, as their parent is unable to meet their emotional needs. Just as children from broken families blame themselves for the reason for their parents' divorce or volatile separation, they also consider themselves responsible for their parents' misery. As a result, they can grow up with low self-esteem and a diminished sense of self-worth.

Note: Of course, there is so much that a second parent can do to shelter the child when the parent with PTSD is going through a rough time and there are many heroic parents who truly do their absolute best in a horrific situation and they deserve to be acknowledged. This is not meant to undermine any of the work, patience, perseverance and understanding that so many parents exhibit when faced with a partner with PTSD and trying to parent children in a house with PTSD. This section just looks specifically about how having a parent with PTSD can effect children growing up and how their adult lives can be impacted.

It is also important to acknowledge that even if a parent has PTSD, there will also be times when their symptoms will not impact on their parenting abilities and they can still use these times to work on their relationships with their children. There are a number of symptoms that are seen in post-traumatic parents which could have negative impacts on a child. These include:-

Intrusive symptoms

Although parents with PTSD may be physically present for their children, oftentimes, they are in another zone. Nightmares, and flashbacks of past horrors can appear by a stimulus which may not even be trauma related.

Loud noise and chaos can send parents into a rage or cause them distress which can be acted out against their children. Even children innocently playing loudly or making innocent noises can be enough to push some parents over the edge. Children are often shunned and ordered to be quiet or they may be verbally and/or physically abused or threatened. When a parent is experiencing a reliving of events, a child witness may believe things are actually happening and get caught up in the intensity of the emotional event and become traumatized.

Children often have no idea what made their parents be in this particular mood, and they are left bewildered and helpless. They find it difficult to trust their parents again after repeated incidences, and an act of unjust rash discipline may lead to years and years of estrangement between parent and child. These situations, though of no real fault of either party, oftentimes becomes a barrier between them, and over time, children will distance themselves more from the parent and will be less inclined to ask a friend home in case their parent is in one of their moods. This only adds to the sense of isolation experienced by the child.

Parents with PTSD may "zone out" making them unable to communicate effectively with their children during these times. When asked a question by a child, they may draw a complete blank because they were not concentrating on the conversation. They may come across as disinterested and distant and their children feel unloved and irrelevant. It may seem like the whole family is treading on eggshells around their parent, and they never know what is going to happen next, and they may feel resentful at the restrictions that are imposed on their life, but guilty at the same time that their parent is suffering. They are often blamed when a parent experiences an intrusive symptom and yet are bewildered as to what they have done to provoke them.

Avoidance and Hyper Arousal Symptoms

To avoid something that brings up bad memories is a natural coping strategy. However, in extreme cases of post-trauma, this could turn into something serious and even life-altering for children.

A parent who is suffering from trauma after being in a car accident could refuse to drive their children to and from extracurricular activities, trying to avoid driving altogether. The child, who was an active participant in extracurricular and other social activities, may find they can no longer pursue their hobbies and find it harder to meet up socially with their peers. They may also deny teaching their teenage child how to drive or may deny them access to the car for fear that they might have an accident and this can impact on their social life and independence as a young adult.

The child is unable to understand why their father or mother, who was always a big supporter of their hobbies and friends, now shows little interest in their lives.

A parent who has just survived from a near drowning incident can refuse to be a part of any family activity around water, or deny the family from participating in such activities, too. Having a parent who was recently a survivor of a plane crash, a near miss, an airplane hijacking or has recently lost someone in a crash can impose a ban on the entire family on this mode of transport and also impose their fears on others about traveling this way also. A parent who has been a victim of rape may downright deny a date night to their teenage daughter, making them distraught and angry. They may become paranoid when their daughter is a little late in coming home.

With the fear of past memories, parents sometimes demand the ultimate sacrifice from their children, never imagining the wider negative impact and knock on effects on their families. What should be a carefree childhood existence, is taken away and replaced with a harsh message, that you need to keep your guard up and prepare yourself should anything bad happen, and to almost expect it will. The world may be perceived as a dangerous and unsafe place where even kids are not safe to be carefree any more.

Children learn from their parents, and by naturally exploring the world around them, in a safe, secure way under supervision and guidance from their parents. Where a parent has a distorted or skewed view of what is safe and what isn't, they unconsciously send this message out to their children, and unintentionally distort their childhood perception and experiences, and replaces them with something more sinister and frightening.

Some parents suffering from PTSD can be extra protective and anxious for their children, sometimes bordering on paranoia. What might make perfect sense to them, can seem very overbearing and embarrassing for their children, especially children who are growing up and on the brink of adolescence.

As a child, all imaginary play is real, but in a house with PTSD, where they may see their parent acting out and reliving an experience, they become confused with what is real and what isn't. They may feel that danger exists even when you can't see it, or that their parent is acting this way because they must have done something to upset them, even though they don't understand what they could have done to provoke such a response. This is utterly bewildering and frightening for a child.

Parents with PTSD can withdraw from company to the point others consider them anti-social. They can detest "get togethers" and family gatherings and at times seem at a loss at what to do and say to other people. Over time, the number of friends may diminish. Unknowingly, they slowly isolate themselves and their families from others.

Children, very often, learn the same patterns of solitary living from such parents. They may have limited friends and may not be able to invite their friends' home, because they never know when something is going to happen or when their parent is going to be in a mood. Slowly, they can become as much of a loner as their parent is. They may be embarrassed or ashamed of their parent, yet feel overwhelming guilt about their feelings, and this adds to their sense of isolation and desperation.

In some cases, where a parent suffers from PTSD due to losing a partner, children may try to compensate for the role of the missing parent by taking some of the responsibilities of the deceased parent on themselves. However children are not equipped to take on the responsibilities of a parent, and will not get to act as a child does in a simple carefree way. They worry about things that are not their responsibility and become anxious and depressed by the uncertainty of it all.

In some cases, parents who want to hide nothing from their children, and think that they need to know the 'whole truth, and nothing but the truth', or parents who feel that it is their duty to prepare their children for what's out there in the world, give explicit and vivid details of their traumatic experience to their children. The children, in turn, may have terrible nightmares, and the same fears their parents have, as they are not emotionally equipped to deal with these revelations and fear based living approach.

Parents can pass all their fears and insecurities to their children and in return they grow up fearful, believing that every stranger is out to get them and danger lurks at every corner. Their perceived safe environment seems to be ever diminishing, as is their comfort zone. The parents' fears and worries become a part of their children's lifestyles by default.

The opposite is also true where a parents PTSD is met by a wall of silence and secrecy, and the child senses something is wrong, then sees things going wrong, but no explanation is offered, or the explanation given is entirely inadequate. The child's imagination runs wild as they imagine all sorts of terrible things that made their parent act that way. Unfortunately the child's reasoning of what happened may be worse than if the parent was able to give an age appropriate explanation of what happens when it does happen!

It is very important that the other supportive parent who does not have PTSD fills the gaps in parenting and shelters and nurtures their children, so that any hurt or trauma directed at the child, or in the environment of the child is minimized. Of course they should also take whatever help that is offered from friends and relatives, and ensure the avenues of communication remain open to them and their child, and if need be, they have a place to go to where they can feel safe.

Older children, especially adolescents and teenagers, will tend to be more confrontational and rebel more against their parent, even if they are silently rebelling, a parent going through PTSD can pick up on this, and may direct their rage or paranoia at them, and there may be "full-on" confrontations or verbal slinging matches exchanged between them, which intensifies the whole experience for everyone living in the house.

The atmosphere can be one of raw emotion and hostility, and leads to significant emotional breakdown. The children may try to emotionally distance themselves from the parent, or numb themselves from the experience, but are devastated by what it is doing to their family, and feel horrible and remorseful or guilty at the same time. By numbing themselves, they may withdraw on all levels, until they almost disappear from the radar, so they almost fade in to the background. They become part of a group of invisible sufferers of a very terrible tragedy that fills them with intense fear and loss.

Children may try to prove their strength inappropriately by lashing out at siblings, friends or by trying to overachieve at physical levels. There may also be problems at school where the child will be punished for their behavior, even though sadly their behavior is a severe side effect of growing up with a parent with PTSD and the legacy it has passed down to them. Unfortunately families with PTSD, can show more heightened negative emotions, disconnection, lack of structure and support and ongoing power struggles.

For children, living becomes more "survival based" where they feel the only person they can rely on, is themselves, but unfortunately at a young age, children are not equipped to have to fend for themselves, and so they do the best they can. They may start looking out only for "number one" (themselves) to the exclusion of many other activities they should be engaging in and learning from. The can be very reactionary.

War Veterans

Children who are part of military families are more prone to high levels of stress, as they need to deal with deployment and reintegration stresses many times over the career of their parent. There is always the fear their parent won't come back and they feel the stress of their absence. The parent left at home may be struggling to hold everything together and try to maintain a normal a life as possible for the child, but this may not always be possible. They may have to move to a different location and start again at making friends, starting school and trying to fit in.

For any parents coming back suffering from PTSD, it is like they are fighting their own internal war, and unfortunately that war externalizes sometimes too, where they may lash out physically and verbally and may border on paranoia at times. They may see their own family as hostile or as enemies and fly into easily or unprovoked rages directed at anyone or anything. When children confront their parent, problems may escalate, and if the other parent intervenes, they may be accused of taking sides or for not protecting them. Family structure may break down. The child may react by withdrawing into themselves, and feel isolated, alone, afraid and rejected by their parent. They want to help but don't know what to do.

The child may try to find a common ground with their parent and take on some of their symptoms as a way of trying to relate to them, but this is not healthy modeling of behavior and needs to be discouraged by all concerned. Alternatively they may take on their parents symptoms, from the stress of having an irrational, emotional, unpredictable, paranoid parent. Also they may act as if they are in a war situation themselves, and express an unhealthy interest in violence and power games. In other cases, the child may try to protect their parent and "parent them" even though this is something they are not equipped to do.

Holocaust and other wars

Even though the number of survivors of the Holocaust have dwindled, studies have shown that the legacy of this crime remains in their children. Although adults today, they were once children and grew up in homes where their parent or parents were traumatized but were not given the support they needed to deal with everything they lived through and experienced. Back then there was no such diagnosis as PTSD and so left untreated many of their children also went on to suffer from PTSD.

Studies have shown that their children even though they had not directly experienced the horrors their parents had, they lived it indirectly and were found to have higher levels of the stress hormone cortisol. Not only this but genetic changes due to environmental stressors were also observed in these cases and these changes were passed down their children.

The same can also apply for survivors of other wars around the world and for their children growing up today. This is known as secondary traumatization, where the child, in some way, relives their parent's traumatic experiences or becomes obsessed with what has happened, even to the point where they may even manifest symptoms similar to their parent.

Dysfunctional family

The primary goal of any parents should be to raise healthy, happy children who will be well adjusted and make a life for themselves independent of their parents. However for children growing up with a dysfunctional parent or parents, so often these parents are not equipped to do this. What happens is that the child suffers on many levels for the destructive parenting practices of their parents, their significant personal problems, and lack of consideration for the wellbeing and welfare of their children. Instead children are expected to accommodate the dysfunctions of the parent and effectively "put up and shut up."

Although there are so many types of dysfunctional family circumstances, for a child to develop PTSD, they must meet the criteria outlined in an earlier chapter. Of course where the degree, intensity and frequency of dysfunctional behavior, circumstances and conditions are too much for the child to process, the child will most likely get PTSD. Some examples are given below.

Types of Dysfunctional Families

Families where one or both parents are addicted to alcohol, drugs or some other addiction. As a result of the influences of these addictions, parents may go missing, pass out frequently, parent inconsistently and unpredictability. Children from these type of dysfunctional families grow up with unpredictability, financial insecurity and learn to distrust or dislike their parents because they are unable to provide for their needs.

Families where one or both parents are prone to violence or are in a volatile relationship with each other. They may threaten each other or their children at home. Children in these families grow up with violence or the threat of violence in their lives every day, and by default can learn to use violence to get what they want also. Children from these families grow up watching their parents fight, scream, abuse and openly criticize each other. They may take sides in the family, standing up against abusive parents.

Children who have gone through forcible separation from a parent or who have been used as a pawn in the relationship problems of their parents are also prone to PTSD. Where one or both parents try to turn their child against the other parent and try to alienate them from a parent they loved, they tend to suffer from low self-esteem, self-hatred, and depression and if older may turn to substance or alcohol abuse. Constantly "bad mouthing" the other parent, refusing to talk about them, or limiting the child's contact with the parent is deeply traumatic for the child and is a form of child abuse.

Children become overwhelmed and stressed at having to reject or be asked to reject their other parent who has always treated them well. Over time they can lose the ability to give and receive love. If not treated, they are also likely to repeat the same pattern of rejection of their partner and children.

Teaching a child to hate or fear their other parent without good reason is severely, mental and emotional damaging for the child. In some respects, children alienated from a parent is comparable to other child victims involved in extreme conflict situations. Some examples include children forced to become child soldiers and children who have been abducted from their family but in their terror, confusion and sense of abandonment, identify with and relate to their captors as a means of self-preservation no matter how dysfunctional the relationship may be. Of course the longer this goes on, the more damaging the effects to the child.

Parents that have mental health or other problems who abuse their children physically, emotionally, mentally or sexually. They may be continuing on the cycle of abuse they felt as a child or they may have a mental or other disorder that makes them abusive by nature. These parents have distanced themselves emotionally from the harm they are doing to their children. It is all about power play and control and no regard for or acknowledgment for the needs of the child. Their children will always be seen as inferior to them and will be used as the parent sees fit. Although there are many other types of dysfunctional families. Only the main ones that have the greatest likelihood for PTSD development in children are discussed.

Effects on Children

Rebellion

One common way to fight the unhappiness in the house is to rebel against it. This can manifest itself through disciplinary problems in school, fighting, destroying property, failing grades, drug abuse, and teenage pregnancy, petty theft, smoking and drinking. They may engage in bullying of other children and may end up dropping out of school uneducated and without adequate life skills to prepare them for life. They may have grown up with unhappy parents who are in a violent or abusive relationship with each other. They may have witnessed violence and fights and are themselves sucked into them, unknowingly.

In many cases, they fall into the wrong crowd and tend to hang around with other children who are also suffering from problems at home. They may get into trouble with the law, get suspended or expelled from schools, or engage in anti-social behavior.

Children from families with a PTSD parent have a greater tendency to have low self-esteem, be anxious, depressed, aggressive and self-destructive because these may be the behavior traits they have picked up from their parent. Being raised in an environment that is not happy, nurturing or fulfilling, they learn to have low expectation from life and are more prone to suicide. When they grow up, these children have a greater likelihood to enter damaging relationships. For those who grow up having a self-destructive attitude towards life and poor opinion of themselves and others, they find it difficult to maintain a positive relationship in their life. Adult children may struggle to be good parents and good spouses themselves when their time comes.

Seeking perfection

Understanding the need for affection in the family, they shower their parents with love and attention; exhausting themselves in the process. They go to great lengths to support a dysfunctional parent. They try hard to excel in studies and other activities, sometimes forgoing their own interests or aptitudes. They are caring and lovable, and lavish all their attention and love on mending their families. As a result, they are left with almost no time for themselves. They have very few friends and interests in life as they plan their existence around their families. They devote their childhood in trying to ease their parents' pains and sufferings. They take on responsibilities for their whole family at a very young age and instead, lose themselves in the process.

The Loner

Unable to handle the unhappiness of a dysfunctional family, these children tend to disappear into the background where they are quiet, withdrawn and introvert. They are almost invisible to the rest of the world. They are loners and are often ridiculed and bullied by others. These children are usually sad and reserved, and look for ways to avoid reality. They too, are prone to alcohol and drug abuse. They are lonely and are susceptible to attempted suicide.

Neglected by parents who often show great emotional need themselves, these children oftentimes finds themselves more and more unwanted and unloved, especially by their parents, who are supposed to be there for them always. While suffering from low self-esteem and low self-worth, they can become accustomed to having no expectation of themselves or from others, as they may not have received much guidance and modeling from their parent. Children find themselves lonely and isolated, feeling unable to confide in anybody.

The Abuser

When rebellion goes too far, a child can grow up to become an abuser. Years of untreated trauma and abuse where their needs as a child were left unmet and where the only relationships they learned from were dysfunctional ones, has taken its toll and the adult child now finds themselves in a déjà vu type of situation where history is repeating itself.

Even when children leave home and try to put some distance between them and their parents, if their childhood is really horrific, the legacy of what they have been through will live on in their thoughts, experiences and actions. Children may find themselves using words that their parent said to them or doing things that were done to them thus continuing the cycle of dysfunction and destruction.

While adults from dysfunctional families may be successful in their careers and respected in society, they can lead an empty and dissatisfied life. Inwardly, they may still struggle with rejection, self-sacrifice and self-criticism. They may also struggle with what society's expectations are for them.

Unfortunately children can also feel resentment toward their parent who does not have PTSD. They may feel the other parent didn't do enough, or didn't protect them enough from the effects of PTSD. They may also fear something bad will happen to their "normal" parent and they will be left alone to care for their parent with PTSD. This is terrifying, and consequently they may become more clingy and concerned for their parents safety and welfare.

Of course, there is so much that a second parent can do to shelter the child when the parent with PTSD is going through a rough time, and there are many heroic parents who truly do their absolute best in a horrific situation and they deserve to be acknowledged. The dedication, patience, perseverance and understanding that so many parents demonstrate when coping with a partner with PTSD and trying to parent children in a house with PTSD cannot be credited enough.

Children of all ages, look to their parents for guidance and reassurance and they need to feel their parents are physically and mentally present and engaged with their lives, and show consistency in parenting, since children themselves lack these skills. If the rules and boundaries are inconsistent, then children become confused and unsure of themselves and don't know what is expected of them. This is why having a care plan for dealing with PTSD is so important if you are to minimize the impacts it has on children.

Coping With PTSD In The Home

Parents play a major role in helping their child cope with PTSD, even if they are deeply traumatized by what their child is going through. Sadly the consequences of not dealing effectively with childhood PTSD, has massive long term implications for the development and quality of life of the child. A child suffering from PTSD can be permanently emotionally scarred, which has negative knock on effects for other aspects of their lives; such as their education, their career, their relationships, their family and in their overall future. Left untreated, it can lead to depression, substance abuse or co-dependency on addictive substances, eating disorders, and other psychiatric problems in adolescence and adulthood.

However, it is important to remember that there are some things that are under your control and within your power as a parent, and so you should still aim to be the one your child will turn to, look up to and listen to. Consequently as a parent, you can be the best role model for your child.

"A baby is born with a need to be loved - and never outgrows it." Frank A. Clark.

How can Family Help?

A families love and support can do wonders for a child's recovery from PTSD, and will complement any work done by therapists or psychiatrists.

Create the Environment to Communicate

Provide children with opportunities to talk at every opportunity. If they are not ready to talk, don't pressurize them, just listen. They may need more attention or reassurance before they open up. They may withdraw or refuse to acknowledge what happened, or they may become angry. Just keep the line of communication open. As children take their cues from adults, they will be watching how you react to them and to other stressful situations. This is their way of learning, so it is important to be a positive role model.

Sometimes they may not even understand what they are feeling, and cannot articulate it yet, or they may articulate it in a way that may be difficult to understand, but this is all part of their reaction to what happened. However, this is still a form of communication albeit not the most helpful form of communication. Children may feel alone and lost, so it is important to reinforce to them that you will always be there for them. They need to know that you are strong, reliable and that they can confide in you and that you can help solve their problems. Reassure them they are not to blame and that what they are feeling is normal.

Get your Life back to Normal

Even though children may rebel against discipline, they actually crave a life that is balanced and structured. After a crisis, it is important to get life back on track as soon as possible, or to try to maintain as normal a quality of life as possible. It may be harder to do if the crisis is someone passing away or an accident or an act of violence against your child or someone close to you, but try to keep things as normal as possible.

Things like maintaining regular sleep times, regular breakfast, returning to school, homework and playtime. This will keep your child occupied and put a sense of normalcy in their lives so they will understand that not everything has to change! Give them opportunities to make decisions for themselves as PTSD can leave them feeling helpless like they have no control over their life. As they grow older they may talk more or ask more questions about what happened as they reach different stages in their development.

Stay in touch and ask for help

If your child is of school going age, inform their school counselors and accept any support given. Psychologists, mental health counselors and social workers form part of the support service for children in distress. Take advantage of any help offered for how you can cope best and best help your child also. Even if the relationship is damaged, there is still a lot you can do as a parent to repair the damage and to make up for lost time before it is too late. Children should be the most important aspects of every parent's life and should always come first.

Talk to your Children

Children of all ages, look to their parents for guidance and reassurance, and it is the parent's duty to help them through any rough patches in their lives. Successful communication between parents and children will help wash away years of resentment and hurt. Explain to them about PTSD in age appropriate language, and focus on how you talk to them more than what you say, as this will be the first thing a child will pick up on. Get down to their level, use a soft voice, slow movements, make eye contact and speak in a way they will understand best. What you say is secondary to all this. Let your children know that it's okay to talk about PTSD and how it affects you all, and if they ask questions, that you will help them find answers.

Do your job as a Parent

Even though there will be times you want to avoid everyone or are going through something, it is important they know you will still be there for them. They also need to understand clear boundaries so that you remain consistent in your parenting as much as possible. These boundaries instill safety and a sense of structure in their lives which will be even more important during any rough patches with PTSD. Being a parent is a full time job and a childs welfare and wellbeing needs to come first no matter how tough the situation. Be patient and try not to react negatively to outbursts and rebellion as they are just trying to deal with everything they are going through.

Maintain a Structure in their Lives

As much as they resist it, children do crave a sense of discipline and structure in their daily lives. Maintaining a controlled lifestyle in the house will give them the feeling that everything is okay. Even if your personal life is in turmoil, try to maintain a proper lunch and dinner time, a proper bedtime and a proper school routine. Don't forget any regular occasions to maintain normality as much as possible in the household.

What if a parent has PTSD?

Parents with PTSD can help their child cope with the implications of having a parent with PTSD. Even though it may be a difficult to do due to the nature and unpredictability of the disorder. In this case, the help and ongoing support of another parent is vital, or where there is no other parent present, then another supporting adult will suffice. However there will always be some parents who will neither acknowledge the damage and hurt they have done to their child, nor will they have any desire to "help" their child.

It is a parents responsibility to ensure that their child is sheltered as much as possible from the damaging effects of PTSD. When one parent is not feeling well, it is up to the other parent to step in more and be the stabilizing consistent influence in the child's life. It is important not to give them all the gory details of how a parent got PTSD, as they are still a child and need to be shielded from horror, but at the same time they shouldn't be lied to. It is better to just tell them that you or your partner is going through a rough patch, and at times may not feel very well but that they are working very hard to get better.

Tell them that you love them, and that they will always come first with you, and that they won't ever lose you, but that at the moment they will need to be patient while you through this rough patch, or words to that effect. Again, you know your child best and will know the best words to use. If parents with PTSD are not up to having this discussion, then the other parent needs or other responsible adult needs to step in and be the one to explain to the child what is going on in a loving, compassionate, child centered way.

Children are always afraid that they are going to lose their parents; and when a parent becomes distant and absentminded, they tend to get scared about the situation. It is important that you show them that you can be trusted, and that you won't be ever leaving, ever. Your children need to trust you and trust the fact that you will be there for good, so they can go back to being children. Of course their childhood is going to be impacted on some level but knowing this, everything must be done to maintain a normal home setting as possible. Your children must never feel that they are the cause of your unhappiness. Children have the tendency to take the blame for parent's misery, and it is important to remove this idea from their minds.

Have a heart-to-heart with them, and clearly tell them that this is something that you are going through and that they are neither the reason nor the source of your misery. Tell them that even though you may feel bad, they are always on your mind and you will do your very best to take care of them.

Focus on their feelings and reinforce a positive message that you will always be there for them and love them dearly. Gently correct any distorted view of reality them may have and replace it with a calm reassurance. Even if they try to imitate some of your behaviors during a bad patch, explain to them after the event has passed, how bad it makes you feel, and that you don't want them feeling that way-ever.

Especially if the children are very young, it is hard for them to understand that their parents could be having some 'grown-up' problem of their own, and may need some time for themselves. Again, it is important that one parent steps in more and plays their role to reassure and provide stability when the parent with PTSD feels unable to do so.

Coping With PTSD In The School

While at school, children are still developing cognitive, reasoning and socialization skills and when subjected to a trauma, it can have a detrimental effect on their social and mental development. Not all children will open up at school, either because they don't know how to or do not want to, making it harder to know what has happened and it is often only by observing a childs lack of concentration or see them struggling at school with things they are competent in, that a teacher may get early clues that something is not quite right.

Whether it is going through a sudden trauma or ongoing trauma, children can feel totally overwhelmed, stressed and lost in a school setting where there are certain expectations made on them and they are expected to comply with a set of rules and standards and this can seriously effect their academic performance. For some children already suffering with PTSD, partaking in a school environment may simply be too much for them, and so they may get into trouble at school for arguing back, being zoned out, not participating in class activities or course work, getting into trouble with other students or staff and doing things totally out of character. If not properly managed, it can do long term educational, social and developmental damage and their self esteem and social skills may be adversely affected.

Whether the trauma has occurred at home, in the school or somewhere else, a student must be given the care and attention they need to help them deal with, and overcome the effects of this trauma. Students will look for structure and guidance so a school teacher or a school counselor can be a significant resource in assisting a child and supporting parents through this traumatic time.

How Can School Help?

One of the most important objectives of a school, beside the education of its students, is to be in tune with its students' wellbeing. Whether a child is being bullied at school or a child is traumatized due to a troublesome environment at home, or something that has happened elsewhere, their teachers and school counselors need to familiarize themselves with any disturbing changes in the child's behavior or activities. Sometimes the changes are subtle, the child may become more withdrawn, complain of physical illness or aches and pains, or become more emotional and it may be put down to other things going on in the childs life other than anything more sinister that would have caused PTSD.

When teachers become aware of the severity of the situation and what is going on with the child, they will work closely with trained school counselors or psychiatrists to not only help the child deal with trauma but to help the child to learn important coping and resilience skills to help restore their well-being and give them strategies for coping with future stressors. Of course, for this to be effective, all teachers and staff in a school must be able to recognize the warning signs and risk factors of PSTD.

A Safe Environment

School must be a place that provides consistency and a familiar environment and it is important that the school authority create a safe and stable environment for their students and have someone they can come to with their troubles. Students must have an outlet where they can discuss their problems and be guided towards a solution, even if it means engaging the services of other trained personnel.

Converse And Work Together With The Parents

Together, parents and teachers can help each other around a child's PTSD. It is important to try to keep a students daily routine normal and structured and there should be open dialogue and sharing of information between the school and home. Of course this is assuming that the child does not have PTSD from an abuse type of situation occurring at home. Parents who are finding it hard to cope with what happened to their child should be encouraged to seek professional help or emotional support so they in turn can best support their child.

Listen To Them

As a teacher, it is important to listen to the students in trouble. Whether they come to the teacher with the problem, or the teacher approaches them with concerns, there should be a safe, and unbiased environment for them to communicate. There may be some cases, such as in the case of domestic violence in their family or child abuse or even problem between the parents, a child might find it easier to talk to a teacher or counselor they trust rather than someone in their family, although in many instances they child will be too overwhelmed, afraid or ashamed to say anything. Reassure the child that whatever has happened to make them so distressed is not their fault. Emphasize that what they are feeling is completely normal and reassure them that they will be given the support the need to get through this.

Take Extra Care

Teachers need to understand that a child with PTSD may need extra care, consideration and special attention in class. They may be more distracted and have trouble focusing in class. They may be disruptive, argumentative and do things or say things that would be completely out of character. During this time they will need more understanding compassion and support instead of punishments. Be aware of certain activities that may trigger the child's anxiety or regression and safeguard against them

Know The Extent

It is important that every teacher and student counselor in a school is trained to recognize the extent a child is disturbed and to determine if the child can potentially be a danger to themselves and to their school, family and the whole community. If this is the case, seek help immediately.

Treatment Options For PTSD

Unfortunately when a trauma is over, it is not simply a case of getting on with life and everything will be okay. What has happened, has left a deep impression on a childs life and they may not be able to move beyond what happened, keeping them stuck in a place of terror, bewilderment, helplessness and vulnerability. When it comes to treatment options, it is possible that more than one of the following options are used to instill the following:

1. A sense of safety and reestablishing trust

2. Coping strategies for dealing with painful memories and for dealing with any of the symptoms of PTSD

3. A constructive way to express ones self and express feelings about the trauma including changing negative or limiting thoughts and beliefs

4. A sense that there is a future for them and they are in control of their life.

5. A sense of connection with the world around them and helping them relate to others

Medicinal Treatment

Medication may be helpful in reducing some of the negative symptoms associated with PTSD such as anxiety. However it really is only used temporarily. There are a few medicines that have been approved by the U.S. Food and Drug Administrative (FDA) that can be prescribed for PTSD, namely Sertraline (Zoloft) and Paroxetine (Paxil). These are both kinds of antidepressants which may help fight some of the symptoms of PTSD, such as sadness, depression, hunger, worry and numbness. In many cases, these medicines are prescribed together with psychotherapy to ease the process. However, medication is not a very popular treatment option for battling PTSD, especially in children.

Non-Medicinal Treatment

The non-medicinal treatments of PTSD are much more common and acceptable for children. Some common non-medicinal treatment options consist of consulting a psychiatrist or a psychotherapist, engaging with licensed social workers, counselors, trauma specialists and therapists. The child's parents, teachers, doctors, siblings, friends and family members can also play a very important role in helping a child cope with having PTSD. However, special intensive treatments are needed for children who show extreme sexual behaviors, drug and alcohol problems as well as problem with discipline and authority.

The following is a list of therapies currently used to treat PTSD. These are carried out by trained personnel or therapists. Therapy is very useful because a child may not want to talk about the trauma which led them to have PTSD but it is important that the underlying reasons are addressed or they will resurface in some form at a later date at a more intense level and impact. Also it is not simply a case of talking though problems as the very nature of talking may cause the child to re-live and re-experience what happened in a very real and vivid way thus making the child more traumatized. Hence the trauma must be approached and managed carefully in a controlled therapeutic environment where the child is helped to feel safe, gain their trust and grounded so they stay in the present.

Cognitive Behavioral Therapy (CBT)

Cognitive-behavioral therapy (CBT) is currently considered to be one of the most successful treatment for PTSD. One of the main types of Cognitive-Behavioral Therapy (CBT) is the Trauma-Focused CBT or TF-CBT. The child talks about their memory of the trauma to a trained therapist and they help them lower their stress level and fears around what happened. Anxiety management strategies include skills such as relaxation, stress inoculation coaching, learning social skills, various distraction techniques, biofeedback training and cognitive restructuring.

Some parents are concerned for the wellbeing of their child during a therapy session, when they are reminded of things that traumatized them. However, the therapy teaches them how to relax whenever they are reminded of the trauma so that they are not afraid of their memories again. It also helps them realize what genuine fears are and what they are not. Parents can also be taught how to continue reinforcing what was learned when the children finish therapy. This type of therapy seems to be very effective for young children as well as for older ones.

Exposure Therapy

This therapy exposes children directly to the type of trauma event that caused their PTSD, not through memory and remembering, but through mental imagery, by visiting the place where it happened or through writing about it. Through sustained focus via vivid images of the trauma, the child's fear-response to any stimulus around the trauma is normalized. However, this therapy is not used for very young children as it may be too traumatizing and again parents may have some concerns about this type of therapy for their child.

Psychotherapy

This is actually a form of 'talk therapy' where the child talks to their mental health professional or therapist about the trauma event, their feelings about it, memories etc. It normally lasts between 6-12 weeks where the child is encouraged to express their feelings around the trauma. These can be one-on-one or group sessions. Family and friends who the children feel comfortable with can also take part in the discussion to encourage or support them.

Therapy begins by first establishing trust with the child and helping them feel safe and letting them know it is safe for them to share this information with the therapist. Then the traumatic event is explored in detail and the child is guided through reducing the symptoms they are experiencing, and helped reconnect again with the life they had before the trauma.

Play Therapy

This therapy is more effective for very young children who are not able to address the trauma directly. Skilled therapists use games, drawings, pictures, sounds and cartoons to gently explore the trauma and to help them with any underlying feelings and emotions around the trauma.

Eye Movement Desensitization And Reprocessing (EMDR)

This process incorporates the techniques used in Cognitive-Behavior Therapy combined with rhythmic left-right-left-right simulations (pendulums, claps or other sounds). This works by "unfreezing the brain' and helps relax and reduce stress in the child. This particular therapy is more effective immediately after a traumatic event, in case of both adults and children and so will not be applicable in many circumstances.

Individual Family Or Group Therapy

Where traumatic events affect a group of people, such as a family in case of an accident or a loved one passing away, or a whole school after a school shooting or a natural disaster, group and family therapies are most effective. All the members of a family are present during a family therapy session. This is extremely helpful as the family members, especially the parents or the caregivers would know best about what their children are going through, and can find ways to help each other later after the therapy sessions. This is also a good way to increase communication that can strengthen the relationship between the members of a family. Also, in case of students of a whole school or a class, it is a good way to approach a whole group who has survived the crisis together. Classmates and peers can be each other's support in later problems.

Self-Help Tips For Confronting PTSD

Look For Signs Of Trauma

Not all children are affected immediately after a trauma. Some of them can handle the stress immediately and may internalize the feelings but will show it in other ways, especially over time.This is why it is important to observe a child closely to see what is out of character.

Create a Safe Environment

Create a safe haven for them so that they know that they are safe and protected. Ask friends and family to come visit with whom they are close to and feel comfortable with.

Talk to Them

Communicate with your child about their feelings and emotions. Ask them questions gently, and listen to them if they are willing to talk about it. If they are not in the mood to talk, don't pursue but ask them again another time. Above all, keep the line of communication open and let them know that you are always ready to listen to them and help them in whatever way you can.

Spend Time Together

If possible, take some time off work and spend some quality time with your child. It could be as simple as staying at home cooking or watching TV. Being close to nature is good for reducing stress.

Try Positive Activities

Try participating in some positive activities with your children, especially something they like outdoor activities which are hard work and exhausting are great for reducing stress.

Try Relaxation Techniques

For slightly older children, try some relaxation techniques together. Deep breathing, light exercise and yoga can be helpful in these cases. Relaxing can also open up chances of little heart-to-heart talks between you.

Reach out for Help

There are many groups or specialists available for consultation in every locality.

Where To From Here

It is easy to become overwhelmed and overburdened by the enormity of the horrors that we are exposed to today as human beings. This is not the type of life we were destined to live, and is not one we should accept. Where there is suffering and injustice, there is also great opportunity for greatness to shine through. For acts of compassions, unity, strength and insight into our own lives and into the lives of those around us who are abused, neglected, forgotten, isolated. We must focus on never losing our humanity or ability to reach out to others or be the voice of the abused, oppressed and forgotten. PTSD takes something away and leaves a state of darkness, terror, isolation and grief. This is even worse when you are a child.

Whether you are the parent of a child with PTSD, or now an adult who developed PTSD as a child, these are not our natural states of being and do not "fit" or belong with us physically, mentally, emotionally or spiritually. Not only does it take time to heal, but it also takes a lot of self-work and being around the right people who hold your or your childs best interests and are there to help rebuild the pieces of a life shattered by PTSD. Again

"Our prime purpose in this life is to help others. And if you can't help them, at least don't hurt them." Dalai Lama

Other books by the Author

Learning To Re-Connect The Pieces Of A Life Shattered By PTSD

Childrens Fiction

Owly Safes The Magic Medicine Tree

Owly and the Enchanted Forest

Spirit of the Forest Helps Owly and Friends

Owly Trilogy

Humor

Mommyville On The Road To A PhD in Parenthood

http://www.orlakellybooks.com

http://www.orlakellyselfpublishingservices.com